D0773364

ISBN - 978-1456531034

ISBN - 1456531034

LCCN - 2011900522

Visit our website at www.myuncleswedding.com

This book is available at quantity discounts for bulk purchases. For more information please email info@myuncleswedding.com

This book is dedicated to my family,
and to all who are lucky enough
to find and marry the person they love.
To my fiancé, Mat, I love you with all
my heart. Here's to a bird free wedding.

Special thanks to Susie Hoskins, Alan Keith,
Ian & Nick Larocque-Hart, Yasmen Mehta,
Lisa Reyes, Dilan Roe, and Claudia Spencer
for believing in me early on and helping
to make this book a reality.

My Uncle's Wedding

Written by Eric Ross
Illustrated by Tracy K Greene

Hi. My name is Andy,
and I want to tell you
a story about my family.

One day, Uncle Mike and his boyfriend, Steve, came to our house to tell us the **big news.**

"Steve and I are getting married," Uncle Mike said.
Everyone was excited.
"What does 'getting married' mean?" I asked.

"Well," said Uncle Mike, "when two people really love each other, and decide they want to spend the rest of their lives together, they get married."

"That's right," said Steve. "We're going to have a big wedding ceremony and lots of people will come to celebrate with us."

"Celebrate?" I asked.
"Do you mean there's
going to be a party?"

"Yes," replied Uncle Mike.
"Would you like to help us plan the wedding?"
"Yes!" I shouted. "I love parties!"

We started planning the next day.
"First we need to pick out the flowers," said Uncle Mike.

ACHOO!

The yellow ones were nice, but they made Mom sneeze, so we chose the red flowers instead.

After we chose the flowers, we had to decide what food the guests were going to eat.

"We should have chicken nuggets, french fries, and milkshakes," I said.

"That sounds good," replied Uncle Mike, "but I think we need to have a grown-up menu at this party."

In the end, we decided to have steak and fish, but I still think everyone would have preferred chicken nuggets, french fries, and milkshakes.

The next thing we needed to do was decide what cake to eat. There were lots of different flavors to choose from!

There was chocolate, vanilla, coconut, banana, coffee, almond, strawberry, raspberry, blueberry, blackberry, mango, orange, cherry, carrot, and lemon.

I had to taste them all. It was a hard job, but somebody had to do it.

Mom said I had to wear a new suit for the wedding. I tried on lots of different sizes before I found one that fit.

This suit was too big.

This suit was too small.

This suit was just right!

Finally, it was time for the wedding. My sister, Sara, wore a dress and she looked just like a princess. I told her she had to kiss a frog so it would turn into a prince, but she didn't believe me.

Sara was the flower girl.
She walked down the aisle and
spread petals all over the ground.

I was the ring bearer. When Uncle Mike and Steve exchanged vows, I gave them the rings.

After Uncle Mike and Steve were married, everyone was happy. We all threw birdseed at the two of them.

That made the birds happy too because they ate the birdseed.

One bird even pooped on Aunt Margaret.
Mom said it's good luck when a bird poops
on you, but I think it's gross.

After the wedding, we had a big party, and ate lots of food and cake. Then Uncle Mike and Steve opened all of their presents.

They must really love to cook because everyone gave them pots and pans.

The DJ played really good music. Uncle Mike and Steve showed me all the cool dance moves. We were the best dancers at the party.

We decided to take family pictures. Now that Uncle Mike and Steve are married, our family is a lot bigger!

Maybe this means I'll get more presents on my birthday.

I like weddings. I'm glad that Uncle Mike and Steve got married because they really love each other. I used to have only one uncle, but now Steve is my uncle too. I think two uncles are better than one.

The End